KATHLEEN L. O'CONNOR

Embracing Two Lives

A JOURNEY OF LOVE, LOSS AND HEALING

Published by Kathleen O'Connor LLC
2501 Canterbury Lane E., #320
Seattle, WA 98112

ISBN-13: 978-0615483832

ISBN-10: 0615483836

Library of Congress Number: 2011929233

First Printing: May 2011

Printed in USA

Manuscript Copy Editor: Terry Rogers, MD

Introduction Copy Editor: Nancy Rudy

Design: Scott Carnz, Dean, The Art Institute of Seattle

TABLE OF CONTENTS

DEDICATION

Ciara Anne Marie Cullen	December 14, 1972—October 24, 1988
Remi Miles Kaemke	November 7, 1978—December 22, 1991 (author's son)
Scott Page Lancaster	January 22, 1962—May 5, 2006 (son of Dorothy Graham)
Jimmy Madigan	May 12, 1964—December 12, 2001
Amy Cordova Myers	September 29, 1969—September 3, 2005
Merrily McManus Laytner	August 27, 1942—October 24, 2010 (Amy's mom)
Scott McKee	August 28, 1951—December 29, 2009
Christoph McKenzie	February 25, 1985—September 2, 2010 (son of Novelett Cotter)
Luke Rogers	July 19, 1989—September 20, 2008
Charlotte Fiona Sutphen	February 15, 2002—September 14th, 2010

This book is for all of us who have endured the loss of someone we have deeply loved and for all parents around the world who have lost a child. I offer this book in hopes it brings some peace and solace.

Song of Songs 8:6 Love is stronger than death.

April 12, 2011

EMBRACING TWO LIVES:
A JOURNEY OF LOVE, LOSS AND HEALING

My son, Remi Miles was killed suddenly in a car accident 45 days after turning thirteen. Six boys were in the car. Five walked away. The accident was December 21st. He died the morning December 22, 1991. I had spent the 21st buying Christmas presents for him.

This is a book I never intended to write and never would have thought of writing. I thought who would want to go through this hell hole a first time, much less a second, much less voluntarily? Who would have thought these poems and story could bring comfort, not just pain? I am so pleased they seem to be doing so.

I would not have written this if it were not for my new friend Carol Madigan, whose son Jimmy died in December 2001. Carol was the first to read this entire collection of poems. I told her about the collection I was putting together. She said she would like to read them, but wanted some time because it would be like taking a deep breath to dive into a very cold lake. When I had not heard from her for about three to four weeks, I was about to write her saying she did not have to read them, when an e-mail from her bolted onto my computer screen telling me how much the poems meant to her and how beautiful they were. She encouraged me to publish them. Then she asked if I had any poems or writings from Remi. I did and I added them as well.

Based on Carol's reaction and comments, I asked two of my writing friends—Nancy Rudy and Kit Bakke—to read them. They also encouraged me to publish them.

I chose the title *Embracing Two Lives* for several reasons. First, I have two lives. One before Remi died and now one without him. I am not now nor will I ever be the person I was before.

Secondly, I am also what is left of his life and want to give tribute to his. After Remi died the headmaster of his school, Roger Bass, told me a story which has stayed with me. When Roger was 12, his cousin died when she was only 13. Roger said he wondered why she had died and not him. The only conclusion he could come to, Roger said, was that he had to "live my life in a way that would honor hers." That is what he has done in founding University Preparatory Academy and his broad civic work in Seattle, which is where we met in a Seattle leadership program: Leadership Tomorrow in 1984. I have tried to do the same for Remi. I have dedicated every book/monograph I have written since then to him—and now this book.

Roger told me he had never told that story to anyone before. I asked him if he would please share his story at Remi's memorial service—so many of Remi's friends had never had anyone in their life who had died, much less someone their age and a friend. Roger did so. I am so grateful he did.

For the past 25 years I have worked in health care marketing communications. After Remi died, I threw myself into health care reform because I knew the system was big enough and tough enough to absorb my anger. Remi had always been proud of my health care reform work. So getting health care for more people was something I could dedicate to his memory. It was something I could do for him. Whenever things became too heated or I started to worry about making ends meet, I would remind myself that the worst thing that could happen to me has already happened. I kept going. I needed something to keep going.

But, last year when I moved my downtown office home, I found 40+ years of poems I had written. As I was culling through them, I started to gather the poems I had written for and about Remi and put them into a separate pile. Soon I had a collection. Then, for the first time, I shared them. I gave them to Carol.

In looking at publishing options on another project, I learned that publishers do not want to publish a book with fewer than 55 pages, because the spine is not wide enough to print the title. Without a title on the spine, the book would not be visible on a bookshelf. I remembered that I had written a section about Remi in a family memoir I was working on, so I copied that and included it in here as well. And, now. Voila! A book.

Many thanks are in order. My appreciation goes to Terry Rogers, MD, who was the copy editor. His son Luke was killed in a freak boating accident in 2008. Also many thanks to Leslie McGovern, a dear friend who also took the time to read, edit and comment. I tracked down Scott Carnz, the designer of my first book, *The Buck Stops Nowhere: Why America's Health Care is All Dollars and No Sense.* He is now the Dean at The Art Institute of Seattle and even so, he decided to do the design for *Embracing Two Lives.* And many thanks to Nancy Rudy for helping me clarify my thoughts in this introduction.

I did not expect this book, but it clearly wanted to be written. For years I have wanted to write for myself. I now have the time and the funds to continue my writing keep appearing. This book was meant to be.

I remember at Luke's memorial service, Terry saw me come in and came up and hugged me. He said: "Kathleen, because you made it through, Karin and I know we can make it through."

With that in mind, Remi and I now offer these poems and his story for others on a journey none of us wanted to take in the hopes these words will bring some peace and solace.

I learned something important in assembling this. I am now tired of being the determined, intense advocate. I have fought the good fight, but want to move on. What Remi brought to me when he was born was love. He brings me love and writing once again—which is where we started. I need to focus on the love that gets us all through; the love that binds us all.

Also thanks to Rabbi Anson Laytner, husband of my friend Merrily who lost her daughter Amy in 2005 to leukemia. We lost Merrily last year in 2010. Anson is right in adding *Song of Songs* to the Dedication: *Love is stronger than death.*

Kathleen O'Connor for Remi Miles Kaemke

April 11, 2011

I. IN MY VOICE

Poems of and for Remi Miles
November 7, 1978—December 22, 1991

Remi holding Chico on the Canadian River

Melon

I will be around
this summer.
I will be round
ripening
    like a peach
    a melon.
Round, ripe
    and fructuous.

A New Gait   April 1979

The tea is jasmine and warm.
I sip and watch the grey, cold rain.
Rain is a balm,
soothing
like a wave lapping my body.
Rain washes my thoughts.
Tea comforts my body.
    I re-entered today
    that easy former stride
    like re-mounting a horse
    delighting in its familiar gait.
    Talk of processes, sequential order;
    the assurance of composing
    topical and thorough reports.
    Banter with others is easy.
Dialogue with myself
    I find hard to master.
My son wrestles on the floor
engulfed in his world of motion;
fighting himself to learn to turn.

I sit with pen and paper
as I have for ten years.
But, I have no deadline.
Just the tea, just the rain.
Just the blank sheets
of lined paper.
> Old strides, known strides
> are dangerous.
> They permit virtuoso performances
> when all they are
> are old, comfortable.
> Certain.
My son's body knows one day
it will turn over, will crawl, will walk.
I sip the tea, jasmine tea.
Rain thoughts upon the paper.

A Chill   October 1980

> Last autumn
> he hardly knew leaves.
> They were as new
> as flowers or snow.
> Now the trees
> are shedding.
> He discovered the piles.
> Jumped into the heaps
> tossing leaves over his head.
> Plowed trucks and trikes into
> hills of yellow and brown.

Then, quietly, he laid down.
I covered him in
a quilt of autumn.
His eyes glazed, stared
past the lattice roof of branches,
past the shredded
thatchwork of autumn.
I said "Good night."
Then he laughed,
bolted, bounded off
to the next heap,
leaping as he ran.

I leaned back
against the tree
watching.

Dreading winter
and empty houses.

On the Canadian River   June 1984

The Canadian River flows through the Panhandle of Texas, in high plains, is several feet wide.

Morning cracked wide open
filling fields with creeping dew and birdsong.
The pasture grayed to green.
You rode with Luke on Country Cord.
I trailed on Chico with ghosts of Paint and Cherokee.
We rode in stride
on your first ride.

Pay attention, I say, snakes live here.
Deer leap like blown cotton
eagles soar
rabbits jump for no reason
wild turkeys flee from our steps.
Gulp air as you gallop.
Loose your hair.
Smile into the sage.
This is my secret place.
I will have my ashes strewn here
where the land is sleek and sere to the sky.
I'll mingle with bones of coyotes and crow.

But is it morning now and your first ride.
Dust mingles with dew
sage swells with water
smells large as Cottonwood and streams.
We lope on a May green plain of grass
and Indian Paintbrushes.
You will remember the eagle
the deer, the turkey and
how to ride.

And, for awhile I will gallop near you
on my stalking horse of death and dreams
over pastures still long with life.

Ordinary Time   **November 1986**

Ordinary Time comes from Episcopal Church teachings. (I think).

It is ordinary time.
Time in its usual dimensions:

love, death, birth, work
sins and celebrations.
Unexceptional
snuggling between bedtime stories
dinner to be cooked
parties to attend
goodnight hugs and kisses
bills and breakfast dishes.

It is time to find a job
or lose one
between the feedings of the cat.

It is ordinary time
with schools and swimming lessons
and income measured by the outgoing pit.
Soccer matches and basketball
between the feedings of the cat.
And love's sudden intervention
with sumptuous delight.

It is ordinary.
Time.

Time to contemplate
what are choices or dictates of demons
Laundry
Friendship
Walking of the dog
Marriage
Divorce
Anger and tenderness.
Between the feedings of the cat.

If the world is made of glass
I know its shatterings
and sort the shards
with laughter in my tears.

It is without exception.
It is ordinary.
Time.

Prairie Storm

Sept. 1990

Kiowa National Grasslands Texas/New Mexico

Over summer plains
chartreuse from storms,
ebony skies spit
forked electric
tongues.

My city fear was vast
for I could not remember
if a car was safe. No towns
to stop in safety. Just the blacktop
the prairie storm, my son, and me.

Plains spread, melt into sky
space between land and air
blurred.
Clear, open, capricious land
you can watch rain five miles away
as you stand in the sun.
Watch hail crush your crop
while it's dry across the road.

And, always the wind
churning the sky
swirling topsoil into dust
filling the world
with grit.

Wind grinds homes and town to dirt.
Banging doors and useless fences
surrender, swinging as tumbleweeds
into eternal sweeps.

"Let's race the storm!" I said.
When he asked if I was afraid
I lied. "Don't be silly."

Black cobra hooded clouds
sent splitting, seeking fingers
exploding
into sundering cracks of thunder tongues.
Struck the pewtered windmill
beyond huddled cattle.

I drove. We listened to
a book on tape of growing up
in Rhodesia with horses.

Then
at the storm's edge
a last beam of light
flooded a glowing plain
and

eight pronged-horned antelopes
raced on a grass green plain as high spring.
Running beyond all fences
over unmeasured time.

And he saw the raw fury of a storm.
measured with the sun's golden glow
bursting on onyx skies.

Saw antelope fly on grass
green as all beginnings.
Felt thunder
and the magic of the plains
Perhaps heard
their Sirenic call.

Winter Solstice   **December 22, 1991**

Write it.
Blood.
Blood in your ears,
smeared on your tender face.
Tubes stuffed down your throat
whizzing minutes of your life.

Write it.
Nothing left.
Only gag and cough.
No reaction to light
in your once shining eyes.
Your hand squeezed
only once
when I grasped it.

They said you
could still hear,
for all they knew.

So I talked.

They asked me how many
children did I have
as if you
were an exchangeable
part.
Replaceable.

And, only your heart
beat, unyielding
beating, beating, beating
against inevitable time.

I could not hold you,
Cradle you.
Tubes whirred
from your leaking body,
fluid halos, tape wrapping you
shielding you, armoring you
distant warrior against hope.

They said you could hear.

So I talked.

I forgave you for
doing something
you knew I would
not like. Forgave you

for lying this morning.
What did it matter?

I told you as Hans died
he sat up, smiled and said:
"So that's it. The invisible!"
Even though he did not believe
in life after death.
So you should
not be afraid.

I told you, you would see
Claudio and Great Aunt Nell and they
would be glad to see you again,
would welcome you,
introduce you to my grandparents
who would welcome you as my son.
And, Murray would be there too,
Godmother Maxie's husband who
lit Christmas tree candles—German style—for you
with a bucket of water in reserve.
Just in case.

So, it would be safe
for you to go.
There would be
that much love there
to greet you.

And, all I had was words.
Like I was telling you
a bedtime story
when you were still

young enough to
want one.

I told you
I did not want you to go.
But, that you would not
want to stay.
You could not be you
even if we could save you.
You would never walk again.
Or laugh. Or write a rap song or story.
Climb the stairs or shoot hoops.
Hit a home run or walk Julie.
Feed Peepers.
Hold hands with, or kiss Dana.

Write it.
Blood.
The tubes whirred
machines beeped
each beat of your
youthful heart
measuring the seconds
of your too short.
Life.

I told you about
our rides in Texas
and the summer prairie
when we outraced the storm.
And that I had really been afraid
for us.
But what did it matter?

I told you what I had just bought
you for Christmas. And how
I did not want you to go. And,
I knew that you did not want
to leave either.

I told you
if there were ever a son
on this earth that brought
joy, it was you.
And, I was blessed among women
to have such a son.
And how you gave me
the most exquisite joy
I have known.
The gift of my life.

I wanted to yank the
tubes and stop the whirring machines
and hold you, rock you
wash you with cool cloths
to ease the endless feverish fight.
Clean you,
wipe away the pain.
Cleanse grief.
I now know why
we wash the dead.

All the while, I could not cry.
How could I?
I didn't want you
to be afraid.
I said leaving
would be just like

going to bed
so you did not need be afraid.

I wanted you to know that
death would be gentle, like going to sleep,
like when you were sick and
sleep would slip
into healing.
That you did not have to be afraid.

But what did I know?

And, when the drugs slowed
your still fighting, beating heart
you slipped from me
with your halo of shining tubes,
framing you against the dawning sky
filled with
shimmering Christmas lights.

"Nothing Older in This World Than A Dead Child"—*Lao Tsu*

January 1992

Were you once as an infant
as I am grief stricken mother?
Pushed into a strange world
as raw as birth must have seemed?

Now you have turned teacher,
invisible master of your devoted
student seeking guidance
in a strange land.

Your affection shines in
sprigs of spring
blooming full for weeks.
Or in an eagle flying so close
I could touch it. A gift, I think.
Or I hear suggestions
in a language with no words.

I am raw as screaming shock
forced from your warmth
into a blinded reeling world
that once had names and
something called seasons.
Some certain order.

Now, I wail as birth. But
there is no breast to suck,
just the fresh edge of dirt
on an old lawn waiting for
your headstone.

Is eating necessary? Or colors?
I think I once knew objects had names.
Did the world once seem this huge to you?

Whales   **October 1992**

Soapstone: Claudio
     Carved swimmer
     tail raised as if saluting me
     you offered him
     Eskimo soapstone
     in appeasement
     of our thunderous love.

He remains, solitary swimmer
frozen, grey
The color of the death of love.

Whaling Saving
    We wrote everywhere
    Greenpeace, Whale Watch
    Ecogreen and even more.
    Over 10 groups worked
    to save the Whales.
    Friday Harbor had a museum
    with fossils and bones,
    and a phone you can call
    to hear whale songs.
    All for your third grade science
    project: "Whale Saving,"
    with the song
    of humpback whales.
    I still have the record.

Solitude in Blue: Portland Bob
    In solitudes of blue
    the male whale sings
    solitary songs.
    Only the male whale sings.

    You said,
    "Male whales sing the blues."
    And later sent a post card
    of lovers on the half-shell
    eating oysters, drinking
    champagne
    while salmon skipped over waves.

"Too much work, too little pay,
not enough love."
Your last message.

Orca in the San Juans, Washington
You were gone by the time I saw the first pod.
Breeching and slamming into the water.
Jumping and splashing,
a finned roller coaster. Watch this!
A belly flop, up and on the side, a cannonball
A watermelon. Just doing.

Their spray rose like breaking surf
exploding
clouds of mist, rolling
cow and calf, cow and calf
calf and cow.

I called to you "Kiddo.
Look at them, just look.
They're jumping, they're flying."

But you were gone.

The Gray Whale, Carmel, California
At first glance it skittered
along the sea surface
an elfish cloud
so low, so misty
so quick.

It exploded into a gray whale.
lunging toward the sky
flopping back on the sea.
But in July?
Gray Whales are in Alaska
by May.

Another cloud sneaked
across the bay.
Again the whale
rolled out
slamming into the spray.

And was gone.

Next day the low cloud
scampered again above the surf
teasing, here he comes.

And he belted out of the water,
rollicking, full and steady,
unseasonable gift, calling:
"Mom, it's me, mom it's me, mom it's me."

Annunciation   April 1992

The Angel of Death
stretched her wings
spread them in leisure
preparing her flight.

She left in slow measure
wings rising
blue sky silver

shining on dawn winds
that caught her wings,
held her circling gently
down from where heaven
moves from realms of God
and souls re-meeting
through vaporous transformations
to her earthly form.

She found her shape and flew
to you as Cockatiel
color of the evening sky
head of morning sun
cheeks of harvest moon orange.

She flew straight to you,
you, who always wanted a bird,
from the sky to your shoulder
so you could prepare.

She walked your room
arms and shoulders,
chewing her way
through your hair,
books and whatever shined,
tasting your life
while you packed
the final parcels of your days.
Telescoping time.

God and death chose you.
Flew to you as a bird
crowned with a head of sun
and cheeks of moon.

Body steel grey.
Color of the end of light.

Hyper Drive Space   1992

When you were three
I framed my favorite
of your paintings.
Palmier and Prissure,
your 'imaginary friends'
Tall as towers
crowned with halos
of red and blue.
Flowing, draped
in clothes hued
in the burst of all skies.
(My friends, remembering Picasso, called it your
'penis period' because of their shape).

Next to them
you told me
I was the first stick figure
with you as the
box in my belly.
Being escorted to earth
by the other two
Han Solo and Princess Leah.
One figure turns toward us,
another more stooped
turns away.

So
your drawing has always
had a place of honor.

I remember once sitting on
either Palmier or Prissure,
apologized profusely;
served them yogurt
several times at your request.
They were that important.

And, how we needed those escorts,
for your life was nearly snuffed
at birth from a long strangling
unending contraction.
These otherwise nice people,
Flipping me over several times to get
Pressure off you.
The anesthesiologist suddenly
at the door.
But, we survived those 24 hours.
You were carved forth, unscathed
with a frown that all said
matched mine.
"He has your frown."
The first words I heard
to know you arrived safe.

Then, in the swiftness of screeching
brakes, worn tires and the hurtling
of metal, rolling smashing into
the finality of concrete barriers,
shattered glass, whipping bone
crunching collision
from which you never woke.
You left in half the time
it took you to arrive.

Gathering Medicine November 1994

Indians used talismans
sweet grass and sage
feathers and totem spirits
bringing promise.
Gathering medicine.

You were stripped
from me, sliced away
as leaves in a fall storm
simply gone.
Overnight.
Your golden glow rippling
in dappled sunlight.
Gone.
Leaving only naked
solitary branches
trying to hold my heart
intact.

Winter grows darker
now near the solstice.
I gather medicine.

I pull threads of love
clutch them. Find old notes
you wrote, find a photo
shining in a drawer. I wear
some of your clothes as if
I could rekindle your shape.
Your smell.
I wrap the solace of friends
like a shawl, an invisible medicine
sealing myself

clinging to what
I can muster.
Gather medicine.

This month was once
celebration—your birthday,
Thanksgiving, my birthday, then
Christmas and the annual
celebration of every mother's
most shining son.

I gather medicine
to ward off
my soul's winter.

Haven   **October 1994**

It all really started with the moon.
The full moon burst from the mountains.
Golden pumpkin harvest
almost as red as blood.

> This was a place I chose,
> not a place I took in pure flight.
> I had sorted your clothes
> donated your toys
> smashed with my hands
> all the dioramas you built.
> I packed some of your
> clothes and shoes
> in a suitcase so I could smell you
> if ever I forgot. Packed you
> into what could have been
> a weekend with your father.
> Only now it was forever.

I didn't know where
I wanted to go.
So I came here with
the remnants of you
I could muster.
What scraps
of you I could keep.

And, then there was the moon.
Hoisting itself through the sky
moving, rising, floating
with celestial certainty,
ripe and full into my room.

And from the moon, I discovered
sunrise.
The brief sliver of dawn before rains
fogs or sunlight
when orange and yellow and pink
of clouds announce the day.
The birds sing up the sun
warble their success.

> I finally found the sparrow tree
> where they gather to celebrate
> their deeds of the day
> plan where to venture tomorrow.
> The song tree.

And, now the rocking chair.
Not a rocking chair on runners. But a mechanical chair
sliding back and forth, that I can lean into and release the
hunch of the day.

Too boring for you.
A refuge for me.

Now I sit in the morning
listen for the sparrows
the swallows, the finch.
The sky meanders from pink to red
to orange then bright
as the sun ascends.

I watch the city fade from night and freeways
crystalline arteries pumping life
to and from the city, the heart of the metropolis.
The guts of my day.

Now, at night, I return from the pulsing city,
watch the shape shifting moon and am surprised
that such a thought as peace emerges in my life
that you are still with me and let me
find this space.

Valerie   **April 26, 1995**

Morning had burst. Sun dancing, birds cheering;
Awake at an unaccustomed early hour, I woke
listening to birds celebrate.

Then the wail. The piercing lament.
Three stories down.
"Valerie, don't die. I want to die." Wails
knife cutting the cord of life. "Don't die.
Valerie, don't die. I want to die."

You died. I wanted to die.
Not to wake up
to the daily hollow:
Your absence.

"Don't die, Valerie. I want to die," he moaned.
And all I could do was watch. He sat on the curb,
rolled on the sidewalk, threw himself back, rocked in his grief.
But, he couldn't die. He willed it, but
grace would not give that gift.

It is now four years. I wanted to die.
Not to have to wake to cavernous mornings.
Not to have to hear empty banisters.
Not to have to hear silent showers.
Not to have to face no one saying:
"Hey, Mom, what's for dinner?"

And then Oklahoma City
the frenetic ripping bomb.
Faces mirrors of my own.

But, now I am here.
I can't die. Not yet.
It's so easy to die
so hard to live.
I have just started to want to.

What do we do with Grief
when it stalks our heart
hammers it into granite
uncarved stone? Crushes it
into an anvil so it can absorb
more blows?

What do we do with Grief
when it chokes our heart
as an unending, relentless vine
so it aches to breathe, walk or talk?

What do we do with Grief
when it drags us unwillingly
uninvited to dance only with
sere rustling leaves on
glassy shards and brittle
fallen branches?

Yet, I would cheat us
without Grief. Float
unsuspended, unsupported
as fog, vapor.
Evaporate.
Leaving no trace of us.
Traceless, graceless
ethereal vague.
When we were not.

And so, Grief, I'll dance with you.
Embrace you, name you
surrender
the remnants of my heart

so I can savor
so I can recall
what once held my heart in joy.
Remember how my heart would race
outpace my legs, would fly
above rainbows and stars
nest in honey hued leaves
with dawning joy
in awe of my shining son.

So, Grief what I will do with you is dance.
For awhile.
Dive into you
twine briefly into you
And wail.

As if my heart were burning
sliced open
mirroring when my heart
once laughed.
I'll kiss you, trace you
rock in your feverish, but
temporal trance.

For you are just the mask
the cloak, the nocturnal
unspeakable twin
Of all I brightly loved.

A Family History According to Cars
From Portraits for Miles

Grandpa Stockwell drove his 'Banana Car.'
Always he bought sunshine yellow
Cadillacs.

Great Uncle Joe bought
Great Aunt Nell a white
Cadillac every year for Christmas.
He drove it.

Jack in Texas buys
his wife, my cousin Jacquie, a
Lincoln Continental Town Car
every year as a surprise.
They use it largely to herd
horses into the corral
or going back and forth to the bank in Amarillo.
A two hour drive each way.
He got tired of the drive and opened
a branch at home in Texhoma.

Great Aunt Clarisse hanged herself
while Uncle Norman went with Grandpa
in the yellow Cadillac
to buy a car to drive back to Texas.
A return she could not face.

Dad's Robin's Egg Blue Mercury
gave out on the rolling hills of Kansas.
He bought a Candy Apple Red
Chevy convertible with a Continental Kit.

A blazing frame for
blond wife, blond daughter and
two standard poodles:
Billboard perfect family.

My father bought my mother
a 1970 Pepto Bismol Pink
Cadillac Convertible. They drove
their beige VW Bug to Ohio to collect it.
Towed the VW home behind
so they would have two cars.
Dad drives Miss Pinky.

Before you were born we had a rebuilt
1957 VW Bug. A collector's item!
Someone stole it from in front of our house.
Insurance settled for $125.

My Chevy Impala Convertible was smashed
by a Camper driven by a pregnant woman.
We replaced it with a Bronze Buick Sabre Convertible
with what felt like turbo drive!
I named it Scarab.

I got only two looks when I had the top down
when you were an infant buckled snuggly
into your safety car seat:
"Way to go!" or "What kind of mother is she?!"

Now, Aunt Clarisse is dead.
Jack drives a pick up since they own the bank in their backyard.
Uncle Norman, Uncle Joe, Aunt Nell and my grandfather are
dead.

My Dad drove Miss Pinky until his death.
I had to take it from my mother after her stroke.

Now, years after your convertible infant seat
kept you safe.
I would I never know the car
that killed you.
Or the driver.

These Little Things   July 2002

In these eleven years
since your death
I would have thought
I would be more prepared.

Instead, I burst
into tears when
I found a box
in my open storage
room with the view
of the lake and fireworks.

I reached to move
a box.
My breath sucked away.
It was my mother's suitcase
but it was your baseball card collection.

It's the little things
that trip me up.
Finding your smiling face
stuffed in envelopes
in my parents' basement.

I fish in my jewelry box.
Instead of my Rotary pin
its your wolf badge from Cub Scouts or
the paper-mache necklace
you made for me
one Christmas.

The odometer hit 91,626
this month.
It had not reached 5,000
when you died
four months after we bought it.
My first new car.

You're still here
in an endless game of hide and seek.
Darting in again
unpredictable,
constant
as grief
as love.
as thanks.

The Finch   **Mother's Day, May 2003**

"I don't sing because I'm happy. I'm happy because I sing."
                                    —*From a New Yorker cartoon*

I have turned off Beethoven
to hear his song, melodic
red-headed courter.
He flits on Finch patrol
from the mountain laurel
by the upper deck off the lawn

to the pine at the corner of the living room.
Song-claiming his territory.
Not a chirp or twitter
but a weaving, reeling, vibrant
"You're dealing with me!" trill
four times his size.

I pay special attention to birds
since the Cockatiel chose your shoulder
ten weeks before you died.

The next year a frowzy little bird
caught my attention in DC
for the Clinton's first Inaugural.
Tickets I imagine you somehow
negotiated
in partnership with Shirley
who insisted I take her
Mink coat.

That same night complete strangers
included me in their private invitation
to a no media, no press, no strangers
prayer service for the Clinton's and the Gore's.
The eve before their first inauguration.
In the church where Jimmy Carter taught
across the street from my Best Western hotel.

The Flicker at the cemetery
called out twice today
though I could not spot him.

I feel protected by
my red-breasted Finch guardian
(red as any S for superman shirt
you wore)
boasting the reach of my home
I come with his territory now.
Wrapped in the smile of his song.

Flicker

A Flicker grasped my downtown window,
stared straight at me.
Turned and ricocheted to a garage roof
two blocks away.

Flickers live in forests
depend on grubs in timbers.
Not urban dwellers.

Messenger?

The first was Cockatiel
that flew to your shoulder.
You who always wanted a bird.

Golddigger nibbled
your necklace, my earrings
anything that glittered.
Chewing the last days
of your life.

In DC a year later
a blowsy, frowsy bird
ruffled and collected itself

so vigorous I noticed.
"What a strange bird!"

That night I ended up
in a private prayer service
for the Clinton's and the Gore's.
I had no ticket. Strangers took me in.
I ended up in line because
my cheap hotel was across
from the Church where
President Jimmy Carter taught
Sunday School.
And, I was wearing Shirley's
Mink coat. She made me take it!

Years later, working on my book
challenging the American public to have a voice,
Marlene, my assistant and I talked in my parking lot
as she was planning to leave for Alaska.

We ducked from
a diving form headed toward us.
Parrot with clipped wings
landed at our feet.
From where? It couldn't fly.
He missed. Hit the ground.

No mention of missing parrot
with SPCA or papers. Like the Cockatiel.

Marlene took it to a shelter.
She did not drown on the Alaska trip

in Brian's home made canoe.
I am still here to write.

So, I get it Flicker.
Pay attention.
To What? To what?

II. A SONG FOR MY SON

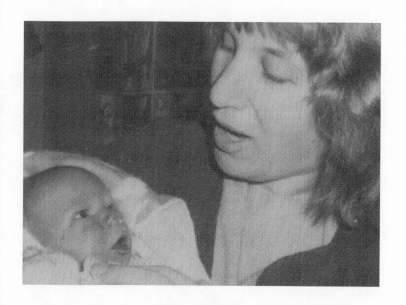

Remi Miles and Kathleen —5 days old—11/12/78

How do you write of a life too short? Where to start? I had really never thought about being a mother. I wasn't great with children and found them more annoying than interesting. But, one year about 10 years into my marriage, I woke up literally craving a child.

Being a mother was never high on my priority list. I wanted a career, so when I finally decided I wanted a child after all, I was thirty-four and thought I would simply fit him into my career. Remi Miles was born November 7, 1978. We almost didn't make it.

We named him Remi Miles Kaemke for Remi Nadeau my great, great, great grandfather who had the 20 mule teams. All the male children in my father's family end up being a Remi: my father, Remi Charles; his cousin, Remi Allen, his son, Remi Robert; and my son Remi Miles. Doug and Claire's daughter recently had a new Remi— Remi James.

We chose Miles for Miles Davis. We liked the name Miles and Ernst loved jazz. Ironically, they died the same month and the same year. Some of our friends thought we named him after Remy Martin brandy. We were given seven bottles by friends as birth gifts!

Interestingly, all these Remi's were pilots, which Miles wanted to be as well. We always called him Miles, but in fifth grade, he switched from Miles to Remi, a transition I never made, but must here to honor him.

I thought whatever came out would have his father's black curly hair. But after 24 hours of erratic labor, one contraction lasting an alarming (5?) minutes nearly killing him and me—he was born by C-Section. As the nurse cleaned him off taking him to the nursery while I headed into recovery, she looked at me and said: "He has your frown." Later people would ask me if I cloned him.

Remi had hazel eyes and blonde hair and was a double of my father as a child. Their childhood pictures are interchangeable. Going through some family pictures recently left me breathless when I found a picture of my father on the beach as a young man. It was pure Remi—in looks, build and attitude. A stance I have often had as well. Cocksure some would call it, I think.

What I was not prepared for was the vast expansiveness of love. I moved so much as a child. There were no constant grandparents, no brothers or sisters. Few deep attachments. So my world was emotionally compact. Constantly on the move. Form ties; leave ties. A year to a year and a half at the time. "Crying never helped," they said.

I do remember an exchange with my father many years later, when he told me that my trouble was that I didn't sip life, I gulped. And I replied, if I didn't gulp, Dad, I would have no life, no connections.

My parents were their own world. Cousins, aunts and uncles were episodic, depending on where we moved. My marriage was not so much one of love, looking back on it now, as it was a 'fated arrange-ment' in my eyes. Ernst's parents never married in World War II, and I had lost a child to adoption. He was smart, funny and good looking and not at all like a lot of jocks I met in college. He was German. We have gone through our angry ups and downs. I have no intention here to denigrate him. He has been hurt as much as me. What we share to this day is our love of our son; the pain of his loss.

When Remi was born, I never knew you could love something so completely. I threw myself into motherhood as wholeheartedly as Remi threw himself into the world. He was in constant motion, as if he knew what was ahead and that he had to gulp life to fit in as much as he could in a short period of time.

Remi had an urgent internal ticking clock. He did not sleep. He wasn't sick or colicky. He just did not sleep. (Until be became a teenager and was impossible to get out of bed!). He would take three half hour naps during the day and did not sleep through the night until he was over a year old. The one dead give away indicator that he was not feel-ing well was that he took naps and wanted to sit and be cuddled.

He was also a 'community' child. Many of our friends were DINKs (Double Income No Kids). For a child without relatives, cousins, brothers or sisters, he was loaded with 'adopted' aunts and uncles and the world's best Godmother, Maxi South from Germany like his father and Jay Jackson, a friend from college who threw himself into Godfather with gusto. Auntie Karen and Uncle Jerry lived down the street and he was loved and surrounded by a family as real as biological, just without the frays. Many of his firsts were at their house—first crawl to first 'date.' Karen even put 'stuff' in his hair so he had a Mohawk!

Remi never really crawled. As he was learning to turn over, one time he balanced himself on the back of his feet and the back of his head and moved around like a little inchworm. I can't remember how many months he did this, but he never crawled on the hands and knees like other babies. The back of his head was bald like a novice monk from his distinctive 'gait.' Maybe this was so uncomfortable that it made him walk so early. He walked at 10 months and ran thereafter.

I was obviously worried about his neurological wiring with his back bending 'crawl.' We went to a July 4 picnic when he was eight months old and he started his crawl. People stood around in amazement saying they had never seen a kid crawl like that before. A week later when I was out with Remi Miles, I ran into this woman I did not know at a dry cleaner's, and she said: "Aren't you Miles' mom? I don't remember you, but I'll never forget that kid and his crawl!"

Those first months were exhausting as I recovered from the C-section, but once I was back in shape, we went everywhere. As he got older, I had a backpack, and we would take long walks. But he would not just sit in it and watch the world go by. Instead he would 'post' in the backpack as if he were riding an English saddle. The backpack was also his stash for whatever plant was within grabbing range. I was simply the pack horse getting him from one adventure to another.

He was in constant motion and I threw myself into motherhood in ways that I never imagined. I had been a tomboy as a child and was having a blast as a mother. "Kids and clothes are washable" was my approach to puddles and other messes, like diving into autumn leaves.

One time when a friend was over visiting, the house became too quiet. I left the kitchen and found him in the middle of the fireplace, covered with soot and ashes. I pulled him out, gave him a huge scolding, and rushed back to the kitchen to laugh my head off he was such a mess and looked so funny. We did, however, get a barrier for the fireplace after that.

My car at the time was a bronze Buick convertible with white leather interior. Sometimes in the summer, I would put Remi in his child car seat and strap him and the seat in securely, then put the top down on those few Seattle days when you can do so. Whenever I did so, I got two looks from people: "Way to go!" or "What kind of mother is that?!" We were that adventurous.

I loved being a mother. I loved the chaos of it. The banging of doors and feet thundering up and down the stairs, the aquariums, the dog, the cat. Even 'Golddigger' the cockatiel that flew to his shoulder two months before he died. The sleepovers. The adventure of a new soul; a new mind! (Get a load of this!).

For awhile he had two imaginary friends, Palmier and Prissure. We had to be careful where we sat. They also liked to eat yogurt. We enrolled Remi in a Waldorf pre-school for a year. It was a wonderful year and with teachers very respectful of the children. One of the teachers was the daughter of a colleague from the University where I worked. Remi would joyfully run up and down the hall calling her: Mrs. Siff, Mrs. Siff, Mrs. Siff (for Smith).

One day he came home from school with a drawing he had made of Palmier and Prissure. They were two large 'penis' shaped beings. One was bending toward me—a blue figure with a red 'aura' and the other was turning away—a reddish figure with a blue 'aura.' To the left were three stick figures. As Remi explained, I was the stick figure on the top left (with a blue 'aura'), the box in my tummy was him and the other two stick figures were Hans Solo and Princess Leah escorting us to earth. It was instantly and prominently framed! Friends all said it was like Picasso, only it was Remi's 'penis period.' We were that carefree and wonderous.

But, as Remi's world was expanding and billowing, mine was unraveling. Ernst's businesses were not successful—from making furniture to re-modeling houses. I was called back to work about six months after

Remi was born—to work part-time to find a Dean of Dentistry, later I found another half time job. So, two years after Remi was born I was working two part-time jobs while Ernst stayed home and took care of Remi and remodeled the house.

I was exhausted. I awoke one night to the smell of burning flesh on the verge of screaming. In my dream I had been strapped to a table for an operation. I heard someone say, "It's easy to remove a heart, all you have to do is cut the three tin wires that hold it." Then someone was coming at me with a circular saw used to bore holes in floors or walls. I bolted awake shaking.

Finally when Remi was three, I had one fulltime job. On the shelf above my desk was a book titled "*Unloving Care.*" It was about nursing home care in America, but it hit a nerve. I wrote a poem that night and the next day told Ernst I wanted a separation. I did not see how I could be a whole mother without a whole heart, in my eyes anyway. Remi needed a whole mother. I was not whole in that marriage.

Ernst and I separated and then divorced. We both agreed on joint legal custody. Despite our hostility back then, Ernst, I need to add, was always a very good father. I hold no ill will against him. His pain is every big as mine.

After the divorce, I tried to hold things together to keep the house, but it didn't work. I took in some boarders, but the income was not enough and we had no privacy. I finally decided if we were going to have a new life, we should move and start a new life in a new place.

Because I was newly divorced, I did not have a credit rating in my own name. Ernst's credit rating was in tatters. With the help of a friend, 'Uncle Bob,' we found a place in a neighborhood near him. It was for sale by owners and I could buy it directly from the family, rather than financing through a bank that would never have given me a loan. I had a good down payment because of the sale of the house on Capitol Hill.

Where we lived in Wallingford was not as nice a house or neighborhood, but in most ways it suited our needs perfectly. It was close to "Uncle Bob." Woodland Park, the Zoo and Greenlake. It was also near good schools and transportation.

It turned out to be a fabulous neighborhood for Remi. There was a family on the corner who had three children: two boys—David and Josh—about Remi's age, and an older daughter, Chantel who was babysitting age—hooray! The boys were in and out of our houses constantly, dreaming up games, watching TV, playing basketball, starting on computer games and tossing food down.

David lived kitty corner from Josh and David and while not always in with the throes of things with David, Josh and Remi, he and Remi would do many things together—cub scouts, boy scouts. They spent hours building dioramas of civil war and World War II battle scenes. JR, who lived across the street, had spinal bifida, which initially limited his interaction with the boys. But as his surgeries succeeded, he spent more and more time with them, although not moving as fast.

It was a perfect block for the boys. JR's mom was home all the time and her house sat on a slight hill, giving her a commanding view of the block. And she was a hawk eye. Our street also had a circular traffic diverter so cars could not speed.

We supported each other as families. The first Christmas in our home, Miles and I returned home from Christmas Eve dinner with friends on Mercer Island. On the way home, the 1-90 tunnel going into Seattle was temporarily closed to remove an icicle from the ceiling of the tunnel. As I stopped, the driver behind me used my car as a brake and slammed into us. I had an old Saab station wagon, which was built like a tank, but the impact was so strong that you could see the road when you looked down over the tires. Shaken, we were both fine.

We arrived home, however, to the sound of running water. The freeze we had had for a week was over and now my kitchen pipes had thawed and water was running everywhere into the kitchen and bathroom. This is now 10 or 10:30 pm Christmas Eve. There are two inches os standing water in my kitchen. I called David and Josh's parents, who called David and JR's parents, and they arrive power vacuum in hand and all sorts of plumbing tools. I stood there in two inches of water crying while they fixed my pipes—it was that kind of neighborhood.

I put part A into part B for Christmas for Remi, and cookies and milk for Santa and carrots for reindeer. And a thank you note from Santa, and we had Christmas breakfast with Jule and Arnie's family for Christmas. A true community. Life savers.

For the first two years after the divorce, I had work at the University, but as that grant ended in 1985, I could not find work. So, I started doing consulting work at home, As if I were prepared for it!

Remi had spent his kindergarten years in a small school called Perkins. Because he was born in November, he would have been the youngest kid in his class in first grade. Having been the youngest child in my schools, I thought it would be better for him to wait a year, so Ernst and I agreed to keep him in kindergarten for a second year.

On the second day of his second year in kindergarten, he got up early and nagged me to hurry—he had "to get to work." The teachers, he said, asked him to help them with the new kids since he knew so much. He felt so important and special. He was beaming! Fabulous tactic on their part.

Then came Perkins Elementary School, which was about 6 blocks from our home. It had been a home for unwed mothers managed by an order of nuns. That need having gone, they converted the grounds and building to other uses. The building was wonderful, had expansive, private grounds, a tilth and fruit trees. There was a senior center that adopted the kids at school, frequently bringing cookies and other goodies. There was an art school that taught some techniques to the kids. One of my favorites is his yellow paper mache fish tray.

We had by then acquired a dog and a cat. The gold fish was upgraded to aquariums. That year of working at home starting a consulting business was intense, but it meant we could walk to and from school, Julie, the dog (border collie/springer spaniel mix) could run her heart out on the grounds while Remi and friends played on the small playground.

We were also three blocks from another park—Woodland Park— where Remi played soccer and baseball. In the fall, I would grab my backpack and head to the school. Remi would climb the trees for apples and I would bake apple pies.

Looking back, while I loved Capitol Hill, its spatial homes and tree-lined streets, it was not as much of boy's perfect neighborhood as Wallingford. And, as Remi grew older, we were close to transportation and a Boys and Girls Club where teens and pre-teens could go after school to play basketball and other sports and crafts while their parents—like me—were still at work.

Remi had fabulous teachers at Perkins. His first grade teacher— Ginger Guy, now an author of children's book—thoroughly loved the children. She kept a notebook of the funny things they said. Two of Remi's that she shared with me were: "You should put your money in a bank because it gets more interesting there." He told her some of his favorite flowers were "Don't forget me nots."

In the fourth grade, his teacher had a program we all loved called "oh, DEAR" (Drop Everything And Read).

His first was true love went to Perkins. Sarah was two years older, I think. One mother's day weekend, Sarah's mom Janice, Sarah, Remi and I and our dogs all went to the ocean for the weekend. I think Sarah was 11 and Remi was 9. The cabin where we were staying had a 'sleeping porch' with two twin beds and a double bed. Another double bed was in the living room. When we looked at the sleeping porch, Remi semi-swooned, and said "*This is so romantic.*" Janice, Sarah, their dog and Remi got the sleeping porch. I had the bed in the living room by the fireplace with our dog, Julie.

One of my favorite pictures of us was taken that weekend. It didn't even rain. It's the picture on the cover.

The elementary school years are now a blur of sleepovers, Cub Scouts, then Boy Scouts, heading every Christmas to the mountains with friends to cut down our Christmas tree. Then Godfather Jay starting a new tradition of cutting trees with Jay and his wife Laura and their friends.

Remi was the center of our worlds. Jay would always say Remi was the best Godson a man ever had and boasted Remi was so smart and talented that he would not only go to Harvard, he would win a basketball scholarship there as well. Laura would pack 'yummies for the tummy' and we would go to a tree farm. One of the last things Remi and I did together was decorate the Christmas the week before he died. David Bassett joined us and to his amazement, we decorated the tree to Rap music. The boys drank sparkling cider and I had a glass of champagne. If it takes Rap music to get your son to decorate the Christmas tree together—so be it. The operative word here is 'together.'

Or, we would go to Lake Chelan in Eastern Washington where friends had 600 'anchors' (acres) of land as Remi used to call them. We had the run of the property, had access to the Lake and sometimes there were tractors for some construction the boys could climb on. Paradise for young imaginative boys.

I remember one time I picked up Remi's friend Brendan to go to Bellingham where Remi had been staying with Ernst. Then we headed to Chelan and Bear Mountain Ranch. We arrived at Bear Mountain after dark.

There was this most incredible August full moon, you could almost touch it—it was that large. So, I said, "Come on guys! Come look! Just look—there's no phone, no electricity, you can see all the stars in the world and the moon! Just look," I said in joy, awe and excitement. All they heard was: "no electricity, no lights" and dashed into the house in seconds turning on every light. City boys.

In retrospect, Remi had two perfect places for two perfect times. Although that would change.

Remi had a magic to him. His nickname in the neighborhood was 'Smiles.' One day we went downtown to the Pacific Science Center with JR. It had a fabulous 'science for kids' section. That day they had a special exhibit on snakes and the curator selected Remi to hold the python while the curator showed off what a snake could do. As we left, we decided to play a game of miniature golf. Remi got a hole in one on the 9th and final hole, which was an uphill shot. This meant he got a free game.

When we got home, a man I was dating, showed up on his motor-cycle to see if Remi wanted a ride. I fixed Remi his favorite dinner that night: Spaghetti with clam sauce. One of his more perfect days.

He discovered clams when he was three after he tasted some of mine one Mother's Day. We went to Ivar's Acre of Clam with my parents. I ordered Remi a hamburger, a bucket of clams for me. He tried my clams and ate nearly half of them. That started a new tradition. Every year on Mother's Day we went to an Ivar's Restaurant and ordered an appetizer of clams for him and a bucket for me. His friends were appalled that he would eat clams! Way too gross!

My parents, who lived in San Diego, invited Remi down one time by himself. Airlines let children over age six travel by themselves. I am a very nervous flyer. So, this was nerve wracking for me. I could take him as far as the plane, but I could not come on board with him. As I was leaving, I looked at the plane and saw the pilot do something they never do—he let Remi play in the cockpit. Remi was smiling ear to ear clicking all the levers.

The trip from Seattle to San Diego is just over two hours and non-stop. When the plane landed, my mother called and said all was well and asked how much money I had given Remi. I had given him five dollars. He got off with $10.

Apparently the flight attendants had him 'help' give out drinks and snacks and they tipped him for his trouble. I have never, ever heard of that before or since.

We went to Texas one year so Remi could meet my great uncle Norman who turned 90, then again at 95. Each time I thought that would be the last to see Uncle Norman. But, Uncle Norman outlived Remi. He also had a son who died as a young child because they could not get him to the doctor in town.

Remi loved Texhoma as much as I did. It is on the border of the panhandles of Oklahoma and Texas. One year we flew to Colorado to visit a cousin and her family. Then we drove to Texhoma over land so flat you are suddenly driving 100 miles an hour because nothing seems to move. One time we raced toward a town because of a thunderstorm and I did not know if it was safe to be in a car in a thunderstorm. The Panhandle is a mercurial place. One side of the road was a black sky of an urgent thunderstorm and on the other, the sun shone on three pronged-horn antelope racing on green unfettered plains.

The first time we went there, Remi was in second grade. We got on the plane in Seattle and flew to Dallas and from Dallas to Amarillo. When we got on the plane in Dallas, we were on Delta Airlines, then a primarily southern airline. As we boarded, one of the very pretty blonde attendants said in a very sweet southern drawl: "*Hi, sugar. You're cute.*" At which point Remi was neon red blushing. Then she said: "*What's the matter, sugar, hasn't anyone ever told you you were cute before?*" Putty in her hands.

We went to Hawaii with my parents where Parrot fish nibbled on his toes when we waded on a reef. We added an aquarium when we got home. At a Japanese restaurant one night, the chef asked him how rare he would like his beef—"as rare as you can make it" Remi said, at which point the chef put a pile of raw beef on his plate. The picture taken there summed up the family—my father and I eyeing the photographer with suspicion. Mom and Remi beaming!

Remi collected baseball cards. On our way to Hawaii, he brought his card collection and a calculator and added up his net worth with the help of baseball magazines.

I took him to Washington DC with me in 1990 when our Governor Booth Gardner, whom I knew and had worked with to pass some health care legislation, was the head of the National Governors' Association. The first night there, as we went into the reception, Booth was coming out. "Governor Gardner," I said. "I would like to you meet my son." At which point Booth looked Remi straight in the eye and said: "Well, that explains the phone call!" Remi's eyes blasted open. "Phone call?" he said?

"Yes," Booth continued. "I got a call from a Principal yesterday about some kid skipping school to come here." Remi gasped. Booth and I winked at each other trying to suppress giggles. Remi spent the entire trip home on the plane completing his homework for the days he missed.

Remi was 12 at the time. Too young to leave alone to fend for himself in DC, I hired the daughter of a colleague who was also coming to the Conference and bringing his 18 year old daughter so they could visit colleges back east after the Conference was over. She and Remi spent the day together sight seeing while Randy and I were in meetings. She ended up having such a great time with him she said she couldn't charge me. The day ended with dinner at Hard Rock Café. Another perfect day!

I probably did push Remi's limits sometimes. When we arrived at the DC hotel it was late at night. We did not stay at the conference hotel.

It was too pricey for me. The one we stayed at was in an apparently 'uncertain' neighborhood, as DC blocks can be. We shared a cab with another traveler, and when we got to our hotel, the man said to be very careful in the neighborhood, especially with him—pointing at Remi.

Great, I thought! We were starving. There was a nearby restaurant—the only one open—and walked the block to and from it in the street, not the dark sidewalks. It was a sweet little hotel filled largely with people from all over the world. I let him stay at the motel in the morning and gave him money to take a cab to the conference, with the help of the hotel.

In 1989, Remi told me he wanted to see the Russian Circus which was coming to town. We went. I sat there and wept as the Russian and American flags were carried by the riders during the opening ceremony. A sight I thought I would never see in my lifetime—our flags flying together. Child of the Cold War when the Soviet Union was the evil empire.

After this, Remi decided to he wanted to get involved in more things involving Russia. One of his classmates' parents taught in Russia periodically. She told Remi about the Seattle Peace Theater and he wanted to get involved. He auditioned and was accepted! He was one of the youngest children in the play.

He was eleven, going on 12, and was turning into a young man. When the Soviets arrived as we were asked to call them, he went on his first overnight field trip—Fort Casey on Whidbey Island to rehearse. A group of teens came from Tashkent and were here for a month, during which time the Soviets and the Seattle Peace Theater members would wrote and produced a musical play for peace. Remi would later describe this experience in an entrance essay for University Prep. He was one of the youngest children in the choir.

The first night they were all at Fort Casey, all the Soviet and American children went out after dinner and plopped down on the grass and looked at the sky. At which point the Soviet children cried: "We see the same stars!" Once sworn enemies, we now saw our children meeting, sleeping under the same stars and producing and performing a play together in front of a packed theater. Remi had a single line. "Destruction of the Rain Forest directly linked to Global warming."

Top: At rehearsal for Seattle Peace Theater, 1989
Bottom: David Basset, Erica Shelley, a friend and Remi on his 13th
Birthday—an hour's limo ride and dinner at
Dick's Drive in Restaurant

Top: Remi with his father Ernst and his grandmother Hertha
           from Bremen, Germany, 1989
Bottom: The three Remi's—Remi Miles, Remi Charles and his cousin
             Remi Allen—O'Connor family reunion, 1990

Top: *Grandfather and Grandmother O'Connor, and Kathleen and Remi in Hawaii in Japanese restaurant, 1989*
Bottom: *Godfather Jay and Laura with Remi, 1991*

Top: Remi and Kathleen in Scarab summer, 1979
Bottom: Remi and Kathleen Thanksgiving, 1991

The lead song they composed and sang together would later be sung at Remi's memorial service.

It was also the beginning of his first major crush after Sarah. One day he came home and said he wanted to take Marisa to a movie. I could drop them off then at the theater, then come pick them up afterward so they could go to see Auntie Karen and Uncle Jerry, so they could meet Marisa. I agonized about it for hours. Do I just take them to a movie theater and drop them off and come back? I finally decided it would be okay. And discussed it as well with Marisa's caretaker (her parents were in Russia). They were just going to a movie theater, right?

The big day came. I took them to the movie, bought the tickets and went to have coffee while I was waiting. Remi had gotten all dressed up—slacks and jacket. A bolo tie. The whole nine yards. I picked them up and we went to Auntie Karen and Uncle Jerry's stayed there for about an hour and took Marisa home.

Fascinating. He never asked to do that again—not that anything went wrong. He was getting too old to have his mother be seen with him in public.

But, Remi's life hit rapids in 1989. I got a call at work saying that no matter what, I must not let Remi spend the weekend with his father. Bill, Ernst's friend since high school, said Ernst had been talking about suicide and while he would never hurt Remi intentionally, Remi was not safe with Ernst right now.

Life turns in an instant.

To this day, I am actually not sure what really happened. And I don't want to dwell on it. I think it was a cascade of circumstances, some of which were outside Ernst's control from a head injury he had had as a child, which we knew little about back then. Apparently, he bought a house near Capitol Hill after we divorced. Instead of moving in and fixing it a little at a time, he gutted it, ran out of money and lost the house. That's when he started talking suicide to Bill. I think. I don't know the whole story. The whole story is not the point. He is fine now.

Ernst called me later that week to say that he could not take Remi this weekend because he had to fly to Australia to manage a construction project. Obviously not true.

I was frantic. How could I protect Remi? Ernst and I had joint legal custody. Legally I could not prevent Ernst from seeing or picking up Remi without a court order which would have taken months. I told the school no matter what not to let them go off together and to call me if Ernst showed up—something that could not be legally enforced.

I don't remember how long this went on—months. I think. It seemed years.

Fortunately Ernst's mother arrived. She had no idea there were any problems. She wanted to see Remi, so I let him go to his father's because she was there. My friend Yvonne suggested that Remi should always have some money on him so he could get a cab if things were not going right at Ernst's house. This would give him some feeling of control.

Unfortunately, Ernst's illness coincided with Remi going through puberty, changing schools and my losing my job at the for-profit insurance company (let's just say there was not a congruence of values).

Disasters come in clusters. I tried one time to sit down with Remi to talk to him about his father. Ernst and I had made a commitment not to denigrate each other since Remi was part of each of us. I tried to tell Remi that his father was sick. But instead of being sick with a cold or flu or a broken leg, he was having a sickness in his head that meant he was not always doing things he should be doing.

I don't know if I did the right thing or not, but I thought I had to tell him to be watchful; that his dad was not always making good decisions now. We had had the discussion on the stairs by his bedroom. He burst into tears, ran into his room, slammed the door crying that he just wanted to be normal. My heart sliced open.

Remi had been king-pin at Perkins. He loved the school, the teachers and his friends. They loved him back. Fortunately I bought the fifth grade picture at the school auction. He is in the middle surrounded all his friends (and at least three 'former' girlfriends).

My job at the for-profit health insurance company was not working out for any number of reasons. The nail in the coffin was when I discovered the error that I had I been blamed for was actually made by the Vice President who was hounding me. Pointing that out to her and the President may not have been the reason, but it certainly meant my days there were very numbered. By mutual agreement with the President, I left at the end of December with a modest severance package.

Remi had six more months before Perkins ended. I was a single parent looking for a job. I have always wanted to write, so I had some time and wrote an op-ed for *The Puget Sound Business Journal* and sent it in to the editor. I called the editor a couple of weeks later to see if they were going to use it. He told me to look at Friday's paper. It showed up as: "Without a Goal Health Care Will Remain A Mess."

I was thrilled! Published! (of course it did not pay). And then, I had a very nice job offer from Olympia: Assistant Secretary of Health in the Department of Health. I played ping pong with myself about taking the job. I had just been published and if I could do that once maybe I could do it again. Maybe I could even get paid to write!

I made lists—pros and cons. The agency wanted me. I told them I would not take Remi out of school his last six months of the school. Having gone to far too many schools and having lost too many friends growing up as a Navy child, I would not do the same to Remi. They said I could work four days a week for 10 hours and have Friday off, until Remi finished school and we could move. Olympia, the state Capitol is at least an hour's drive, one way. Longer at rush hour. I went to see counselor to help sort this through.

I made a list of pluses and minuses. They were equal. Then one day when I was looking at my list, I told Remi about the offer the folks in Olympia had made—the four days a week. And, he looked at me and said: "If you take that job, I'll never see you." Which was true.

I actually had a son who wanted me around! I turned down the job and geared up my business again.

Life turns on an instant.

I did not know what to do for school for Remi after Perkins Elementary. A private school, one friend suggested, is like hiring a second parent. "They have to take care of you." Remi wanted to go to Roosevelt with some of the girls from the Boys' and Girls' Club. He would be twelve in November. He had a head start on puberty. Dana and Erica were in every other sentence. I needed a partner to survive the cascading teenage hormones. I would not find a partner in a large urban public school.

I would have little voice or influence at Roosevelt. I needed an extra 'parent' and enrolled Remi in University Prep. I knew the headmaster, Roger Bass, from a leadership program. We applied. Remi was accepted and was offered a scholarship, which is the only way we could afford it.

In his application, Remi had to write about an event in his life positive or negative that made an impact on him. And he wrote about the Seattle Peace Theater:

"The event which had a positive effect on my life was probably the musical play for peace. It was fun to work with the Soviets. It let me meet new people. I was a member of the Chorus and performed in front of an audience of over thousand people and some big names. It made me feel very self-confident.

It was a nice feeling when I finished. It made me feel I myself had made difference. After the performance, about three months, the Berlin Wall came down and Nelson Mandela was set free. It made me feel very proud, as if I had made a difference."

I have always loved this essay—it epitomizes his bright optimism, caring heart and sense of adventure. Who knows? Maybe he was the fractal that set these forces in motion: the butterfly whose wing changed the wind.

Remi wanted go to Roosevelt with Dana and Erica. Instead, he found himself in a private school on a scholarship—no longer the king-pin. Now he was not only a lowly sixth grader, but he was now with kids whose families had money, lived in expensive neighborhoods and could afford the tuition. He would go to school, then come back to the Boy's and Girls' Club where the other kids were like him in terms of homes and incomes. I imagine now, looking back, he probably felt torn and conflicted about where he belonged.

Having been tossed from school to school as a Navy child, I don't think—looking back on it—I realized how hard it may have been for him to navigate this new world. He made few friends because he took public transportation and some of the other kids parents car-pooled.

He bonded deeply with one student, Alec, who I am still very close with and am now officially "Auntie" for him, his wife Tosca and their son, Thomas. They bonded, in part I think, over the hypocrisy of their middle school head master.

I loved road trips with Remi. We always had our best talks on those trips. We took several in Texas and out ran thunderstorms (I was not sure they wouldn't kill us if we were struck by lightening). We drove the Honda—my first new car—from Seattle to Vancouver, BC and back in one day, listening to whatever music he wanted to hear, just so we could talk and drive the new car.

Since we were not face to face with one subject, we could dance about what was on our minds—a meandering conversation with no particular goal. We always got along best on road trips. We made one long last drive before school in fall of 1991: Seattle, Mount. Rainier, Yakima and back. Seven hours. We agreed if he was miserable and University Prep was not working for him this coming quarter, then he could go to Roosevelt. He wouldn't live to get the chance.

In the late 80's and early 90's, basketball 'starter jackets' were all the rage. These were jackets worn by professional basketball teams with the team's mascot on it. Players wore the jackets over their uniforms before they started to play. Remi had several.

He had one that stood out: San Jose Sharks, but the shark was upside down. Therefore very distinctive.

Remi was old enough at 12 to take public buses to school. The alternative was my driving him—a fate worse than death. One day in October, when he got off the bus to walk the five blocks home, he noticed some kids were following him. Instead of going to our house, he went to a neighbor's house through their back yard and came out in front of the house, careful not to let the boys see where he lived.

Our Hawk-eye neighbor Judy was in her usual spot at her window looking up and down the block. She knew the boys following him did not live in the neighborhood. She came to the porch to 'talk' to them. They split. Remi stayed with her and JR until I got home.

This was the first of what would be three 'assaults' in about one month.

Several weeks later, he and David who had been in Cub and Boy Scouts and built dioramas, went to the Northgate shopping mall north of where we lived. If there were ever a kid on the straight and narrow, it was David. You could always count on him. So, while I knew Remi could push boundaries, I knew David didn't. They did not egg each other on. They balanced each other.

When Remi was not back by dark, as he had promised, I called David. He said Remi would not come back with him. Remi had stayed playing video games.

A few minutes later my phone rang. A security guard from the mall said a young man wanted to talk with me. It was Remi. He found the security guard when some kids were hovering around him asking about his starter jacket.

Furious, I called Ernst who had now recovered, to pick him up and talk some sense into him. I was tired of being the only enforcer and wanted and needed Ernst to chime in as well. He did, and I think it really helped. I was not the sole enforcer. And his Dad and I were now a united front, not adversaries.

A couple of weeks later, Remi called from school very excited: "Hi, Mom! Guess what? A cockatiel landed on my shoulder in the parking lot! I always wanted one. The school can't keep it over night. Can I keep it?"

A cockatiel? Flying out of the sky? They are not wild, but imported and probably somewhat expensive. "No, that bird probably belongs to someone who lost it. Are there any signs around the school?"

To make a long story short, temporary turned into permanent as no one claimed it, advertised or answered ads. So, we now had a dog, a cat, three aquariums, and a bird. We named it "Golddigger' because he nibbled on anything that shined—Remi's fake gold necklace, my earrings. It was a trick keeping Golddigger away from Peepers the cat. We had many closed doors. His birdcage moved a lot.

Remi and the headmaster of the middle school were fire and water. The junior high headmaster in welcoming parents to the school had made a point of saying how important these middle school years were—uncertain years; puberty; personal identity; transition from child to promising young adult—middle schoolers, he said, needed a safe harbor in these turbulent seas. I could not have agreed more. But, if something was wrong, however, he turned his sights on Remi.

There is no question Remi pushed buttons. He was a teenage boy— testing limits was his job description. I forget the first incident that set him off with Remi. I do remember the second.

Remi and I had spent the day over at Silverdale with Godfather Jay and Laura picking a Christmas tree. Just as we got home about 6 or 7 pm on a Sunday night, the phone was ringing. It was his junior high headmaster. "Remi has done it again." Is how the conversation started.

I asked what he meant? He went on to tell me Remi had taken a group of University Prep students to visit Alec in the hospital. He went on to say Alec's parents did not want people to know Alec had cancer or was in the hospital. Remi taking the other children to the hospital, therefore, was just another example of Remi pushing the rules.

"That's ridiculous," I said. "Remi and Alec have been friends a long time. If his parents did not want people to come visit Alec they would have told us. Remi thought that Alec would like to know he had friends who worried about him and hoped he would get well."

His headmaster then said: "Well, some of us now have to make phone calls on Sunday night which cuts out time with our families." I have no idea how I ended the conversation. It was probably polite. And icy. Alec and his parents never called to complain or ask us not to contact Alec.

I mention this for what comes next.

The last week before Christmas break, my friend Yvonne called me at work. I had been out of the office most of the day in meetings.

"There was an incident," she said. "Remi was attacked at the bus stop. A group of boys jumped out of a car, stole his jacket and cut him in the face. They punched Alec who was trying to help. This all happened at the bus stop across the street from the school. When the school couldn't reach you or Ernst, they called me. He is here with me now. He is fine, but shaken up." I rushed to the school. The cut was not serious, but Remi's nerves and mine were shattered.

That very afternoon, however, his junior school headmaster wrote and sent a letter to parents saying that the school was safe. The only reason this incident happened, he said, was that the victim knew the attackers. This was not an attack on the school, but on a student who was known to them. I went ballistic. The junior high headmaster had not contacted me or Ernst before drafting and sending the letter. Remi did not know the attackers—but one boy had recognized Remi's shark jacket.

The next day Ernst and I met with the junior school headmaster and asked him to retract the letter since he never consulted us and what he wrote was not true. Then I made an appointment with the school's headmaster, whom I knew. I told him what happened. A new letter was issued saying the victim did not know his attackers. All the attackers apparently wanted was his jacket and they got it.

Remi was now really scared. He had been targeted in three different places by three different groups in about six weeks. Our house was level with the street; we had no stairs going up to a porch to enter the house. His name and our neighborhood had been in a local paper after the first incident.

Remi thought these kids would find him and come after him. He was worried about gangs. Stealing starter jackets like his was an initiation rite for gangs. He was worried about a drive by shooting. Not unreasonable after having been targeted in three different places by three different groups.

I needed someone Remi could talk to. My counselor would not see him, since I was his client, and he could not take both of us. He instead found the best match ever.

This new counselor was starting his practice and did not have an office. I introduced them without saying he was a counselor. They went and had a coke and played some basketball. A true Godsend! Just hanging out and 'hoopin.' Remi looked forward to their meetings. I began to unclench my teeth.

Things were settling down. School was nearly over. Remi seemed to be getting better and things calmed down, except for the phone call from his headmaster I mentioned earlier. His grades were good and he was totally in love with Dana.

Then, out of the blue, I got a phone call from my friend Tyrone who worked at a local TV station. The station was doing a special program on gangs and she wanted to know if I would be willing to talk about what happened to Remi. I said "Sure!" Well, when I told Remi—he absolutely insisted that he go on the show.

I said—absolutely not! I didn't want his face and voice on public TV so people would know who he was, what he looked like and where he went to school. But, he was equally determined. He wanted to warn parents and grandparents about those jackets.

So, I called Ty and she let me talk with the show's producer. They said they had some camera tricks that would block his face so it looked like a prism and they could garble his voice so it could not be recognized. They even gave me a horrible, horrible wig, so I would not be recognized. We went on. I was on a panel. He was filmed, I believe, in the 'green' room where they prepare people before they go on a TV set. He was on with another young man who had recently left a gang. The show aired Friday, December 20th.

Remi was terrific! He asked parents and grandparents not to buy those jackets because stealing them was an initiation to get into a gang. What gangs were really about, he said, was respect. If kids don't get respect at home or at school, they will do anything to be in a gang which promises them the respect they crave.

We went to dinner at Dick's Drive-In in Wallingford near our house, Remi's favorite hamburger place. We came home. Remi called his friend David to come over for a sleep over. They went to his room and the upstairs study with the TV. They were on the phone for hours. Giggling and laughing.

I was so proud and happy. I remember thinking I was so incredibly proud of him. He had learned and acted on what I wanted him to learn. "Give back to the community what you have been given; speak up for social justice; don't judge people by their color or their religion, but who they are as people. Always give a helping hand in return for those who have handed you theirs." He had done that. Magnificently.

When you are up to your eyeballs channeling a child's direction, their push back is hard. At one time I told Remi: "Don't you know what Mom stands for? Mean Old Mother." Seeing your hard work pay off is wordlessly gratifying.

I spent the evening feeling very blessed about what a remarkable son I had. He had bedrock. I was confident now after these past difficult months that despite turbulent teen challenges we would face ahead—that he would make it through. He had the values, skills and grit to master that voyage, as he had demonstrated these past several weeks. He had a great, great heart and would become a great young man. A great adult.

All that evening I heard their giggles and laughter as they called friends, watched TV and celebrated. And planned.

They were in and out of the kitchen. Remi had back now what he had lost leaving Perkins—his voice and his leadership role.

The next morning I was heading out Christmas shopping at North-gate. Remi and David came bolting downstairs. "We're going Christmas shopping at Northgate," they said. I said I was going there, too. I could give them a ride. They said no, they wanted to take the bus. Teenage boys!

In my heart of hearts, I knew what they were telling me had something suspicious about it. They were too giggly, too nervous. Parents smell deception.

But, I let them go. Remi had gone through so much and come out the right side, I trusted that whatever they were cooking up would end up being okay. Remi was with David, who as I said before, was one of the most risk averse children I knew. David did not like dares or other pushing boundaries behaviors. He was a terrific restraining influence on Remi. I let them go, saying they had to be back by five.

As it turned out, this was the first and only time David ever lied to his parents and he went along, I'm sure, because Remi was feeling so euphoric.

At 4:30 that afternoon I was at Penny's buying Remi's Christmas present, I had an incredibly horrible anxiety attack. I never had one before. I dropped everything and rushed home.

I got home. No Remi. No David. Suddenly there is a knock on the door—it's Carol, David's mother. "There was a terrible accident. Remi is at Harborview."

Seattle has a fabulous hospital: Children's Hospital and Medical Center, where they specialize in treating children. Trauma is another story. Traumatic injuries, no matter the age, go to Harborview.

I knew what it meant to be at Harborview. It was not good.

Carol drove me to Harborview. I'll spare you the police and hospital inquiries: Does the driver have insurance? Do you have health insurance? How many children do you have?

The social worker said he had massive head trauma. Only brain stem activity. He was unconscious.

They had not gone to the Mall. They went to West Seattle with a cousin of someone Remi knew from the Boys and Girls Club. They picked up Remi and David at the Boys and Girls Club, so they would not be seen by we parents. They played football all day. Remi's team won. On the way home, a bunch of girls drove by, the driver and Remi waved and yelled after them. The driver lost control. The car flipped. I don't know how many times. David and Remi were in the back seat. Remi behind the driver.

I don't think he had a seat belt. Six boys were in the car. Five walked away.

Remi was 13. If it had not been for David, I would not have known what had happened to him for days. His hospital ID was Foxtrot Doe. What 13 year old carries ID?

Ernst and I were with him at Harborview for eight hours before he died. They told me to talk to him. I know he knew I was there. When I took his hand he squeezed back. Our last communication.

He was not responding. His gag reflex was gone and his eyes no longer responded to light. He would not come back.

How could I help him go? How to give him peace? He had to be so scared. He was so young. I told him he would be okay. I told him who he would meet and how much they would love and welcome him. That he shouldn't be afraid, There would be so much love there waiting for him. It would be like stepping off a plane and into the arms of loved ones waiting for him.

I just hope that was not a lie.

I later learned that his junior high head master apologized to him for jumping to conclusions about the incident at the bus stop; that Remi told his counselor that he could tell me that he was fine and that he loved me, and thanked him for being there for him. Then he went on TV to warn parents and grandparents about starter jackets and gangs.

His last week was as if he tied up all the loose ends of his life, put a bow on them and was gone. Two and a half days before Christmas. 45 days into being 13.

Uncle Bob told me Buddhists believe you don't leave this earth until you learn the lesson you have come to learn. Bob said I was a good teacher.

We held a private service right after Christmas and a memorial service in January at the Museum of History and Industry after school started again. Over 300 people came. Roger, the head master that I knew and liked spoke. He told the students and others who were there that he had a cousin die when he was twelve and she was thirteen. He never understood why she died and he didn't. To make sense of this, he decided he had to live his life in a way that honored hers. He had never discussed her death before. I was the first to hear the story and told Roger he had to tell that to the students. And he did.

David, Alec, Dana and Erica helped Ernst and me plan the memorial service. They chose the music and the speakers.

The Seattle Peace Theater Chorus came and performed "The Mourning Song" from "Peace is Possible."

After all the attacks for his jackets, we reported the incidents to the police. About a month after Remi died, Ray Thomas, a police deputy contacted me to say that they caught a couple of the boys who attacked Remi outside University Prep. Not only that, one boy would plead guilty and testify against the others.

Ray said his whole station was astonished: "Let me get this straight," they said. "The victim is dead. The jacket was never found, and you got him to plead guilty?" "Yes," Ray beamed.

• • • • •

The magic about Remi Miles continues. I suddenly have found the poems, time and money to complete this book on his life; a tribute to hope and courage that he would want.

And the unwanted but gracious gift of finding other parents who urged me to give his life to share.

III. IN HIS VOICE

Selected poems and writings of Remi Miles

Remi Miles and friend's bird—two years before Golddigger, 1989

This is not just my story. It is the story of all who have loved and lost. And survive and keep their memory in our hearts and minds forever.

Second Grade

On Top of a Rainbow

> If I was on top of a rainbow
>> How fun it would be
> I could see miles around
>> And not touch the ground
> If I was on top of a rainbow.

Scary Night

> There was a house on
>> the hill that I will
> never go near because it is
>> a haunted house
> where ghosts drink beer.

Mourning Song   Seattle Peace Theater Song, Seattle 1989

> The spinning earth the grass the flowers
> Shining bright from ocean spray
> They glimmer brightly in the morning
> Racing down the stars highway.
>
> A flash of fate, a flash of mystery
> Illuminating days and clouds
> We are but children to our history
> Living on an ancient world.

Heaven is filled with stars
The sun and moon shine there
Our earth is filled with dreams
Only one life to care.

Heaven is filled with stars
The sun and moon above
So many stars we see
Only one earth to love.

Heaven is filled with stars
The sun and moon above
So many stars we see
Only one earth to love.

Here in our galaxy together
We take the risk to suffer pain
Giving, grieving, hoping, doubting
We die. The earth can live again.

Lyrics: Valdimir Valdimirov; Translator: Carl Sander

Ray 1991

Ray always knew how to laugh and have fun.
He seemed to know how to make the best out of
the worst situations.
He threw the best parties ever.
Everyone who knew him loved him.
He tried his best to get out of a stupid mistake
he made.

Never complained, took things as they were,
Never showed fear.
Always turned the next cheek.

Questions 1991

How can you say life is a mystery?
Every day draws closer to the answer. The
Longer your days the less you know, is that the answer? No
Life is only a mystery to those who haven't seen death.

Hooping (a rap song) 1991

Hoop, hoop, hoop, hoopin'
When I'm on the court I don't just play
Can't you see its life and death to me
with the whites on my feet
Bust a shot with this funny beat
playing this rhyme about
a game called hoopin'
    hoop, hoop, hoop hoopin'
    hoop, hoop, hoop hoopin'
the competition's jumpers are droopin'
    but I'm gonna keep on hoopin'
    with the ball in my hands
    go flyin' above the stands
    lay the jams into the hoop
Two points more now we're leading by four
    might as well just let us score
    more and more points
    explode on the board
    'cause once again we scored.

hoop, hoop, hoop hoopin'
hoop, hoop, hoop, hoopin'
T-Fly the hoopin' maniac
when it comes to basketball I'm a brainiac
damn I'm ready for the NBA
take on teams from Chicago to LA
hoop, hoop, hoop, hoopin'
hoop, hoop, hoopin'
let's go find a court somewhere
hoop, hoop, hoop, hoopin'
(T-fly was Remi's name when he talked about forming a rap band)

Excerpt from University Preparatory Admission Essay

*Part of Remi Miles' Admission essay for University Preparatory Academy.
March 1990:*

Describe an event that had an impact on your life, positive or
negative:

The event which had a positive effect on my life was probably the musical play for peace. It was fun to work with the
Soviets. It let me meet new people. I was a member of the
chorus and performed in front of an audience of over one
thousand people and some very big names. It made me feel
very self-confident.

It was a nice feeling when I was finished. It made me feel
I myself had made a difference. After the performance, about
three months, the Berlin Wall came down and Nelson Mandela was set free. It made me feel very proud, as if I had made
a difference.

And he did.

© Kathleen O'Connor 1978-2011

IN MEMORIUM

LUKE ROGERS

On the web page of the school that Luke attended (Seattle Academy), there is a saying that goes something like, "Not all poetry is written." There were two areas of Luke's life that demonstrated that this is indeed true.

The first was his music. To hear Luke sing was to understand why he was put on this earth. It was through this expression that he was able to give to those around him the pure essence of what he was about. A strikingly beautiful voice presented in a not-to-be-forgotten way.

The other daily evidence of his living poetry was the natural and uncontrived way he had of meeting people where they happened to be, and the way he included them in his wide circle of friends. It was just the way he was. It was the rhythm and meter of his life, and for many, it indeed was poetry.

Terry Rogers

CHRISTOPH MCKENZIE

My Dear Christoph,

I remember well the night of February 25, 1985 at 10:04 p.m. when you were born as one of the proudest, most memorable moments of my life. It was one of several life-altering moments of my life. You weighed only 3lbs. and 12 ozs. and you were so tiny. As you laid there in the incubator, hooked up to the respirator, you were all at the same time most beautiful, vulnerable and very frail. I was petrified thinking that you wouldn't survive.

Every trip to the hospital was filled with fear because I was never sure what I'd find out when I got there. But I would arrive at the hospital the next morning, you'd seem better than the day before and I'd fall in love with you more each day. Saying goodbye to you each evening seemed unbearable, but I found the courage.

It's impossible for you to imagine the pride and joy I felt two and a half months later, when I took you home from the hospital weighing a little over 5 lbs. I remember thinking that you are a survivor, and everything in our lives would be perfect from that day forward. You were beautiful; I loved you beyond words, and I vowed to protect you forever no matter the cost. You brought me a tremendous amount of joy as I watched you grow, and I was so proud of the man you had became.

The morning of November 14, 2008 when you fell ill, and we took you to the hospital, was another of those life-altering moments. We were so ill-prepared for the news that you had Marfan syndrome and had to have your Aorta replaced with a mechanical valve. What is Marfan syndrome? I'd never heard of it till then. How could that be that everyone missed the signs? Your pediatrician, all the doctors – no one caught it? I was beside myself with sadness and worry. As your mother, I always thought I could find a solution, or at least, help you find one to any problem you face. Marfan was congenital, and I couldn't make it go away. I couldn't fix it.

Waiting six and a half hours for you to come out of surgery that night was up till then the most frightening. I thought it couldn't get any worse. The surgeon finally came out and told us that the surgery was a success. I remember well the tears I shed upon hearing the news …they were tears of joy. What a relief! You were going to be just fine. Again, you proved that you were a fighter, and I began to believe that you would be able to fight and win forever.

Then came the evening of September 2, 2010 when you finally lost your fight. It wasn't because you didn't try, because you tried really hard. This was out of your control. September 2, 2010 has so far proven to be the saddest day of my life, bar none. When I was forced to accept that you were really gone, I wondered: How must I accept not seeing your beautiful smile again? How must I accept that your long arms will never hug me again? How must I accept never hearing you say "I love you Mom!" I'll never hear again your sweet voice singing as you happily stroll along. It just can't be that you'll never walk in the door again!

I find hope in the belief that God had a plan for you, Christoph, his special gift to me. Your work on earth is done and wherever you are, I know you are an inspiration and a joy. God lent you to me for a little while and what joy that was! It was my pleasure and a distinct privilege to be your mother and caregiver for 25 years. The angels called for you much sooner than we expected, but you've left me wonderful memories.

You were an amazing young man – all 6 ft. 5 ins. of you. You were unquestionably a fighter. You faced your challenges boldly and with such courage.

I miss your smile. I miss your sense of humor. I miss your wit. I miss your insights. I miss your intelligence. I miss your potential. *I miss everything about you every single day*.

All my undying love,
Mom

Novelett Cotter

ABOUT THE AUTHOR

Kathleen L. O'Connor was born in Long Beach, California in 1944 and is an only child of a naval officer pilot, Remi Charles O'Connor and his wife Lucille. She was raised all over the country traveling from California to Florida and Virginia where her junior high school was the first in Virginia to be successfully integrated in 1959. Her first article was published in *The Washington Post* in February 1959 about the integration of her school. The article ran 50 years and two weeks to the day that President Obama was inaugurated.

She spent her high school years in rural Japan and came to Seattle to attend the University of Washington to study Japanese. She has a bachelor's and master's degree from the University of Washington. She started her career in the Provost's office at the University of Washington and left that post when she was 34 when her son was born. In the mid-late 1980's she started her own business—O'Connor Health Care Communications www.oconnorhealthanalyst.com and spent 25+ years writing and advocating for health care reform. She started two non-profits to do so: W.H.E.R.E. and CodeBlueNow! www.codebluenow.org

She published *The Buck Stops Nowhere: Why America's Health Care is All Dollars and No Sense*, whose cover was also designed by Scott Carnz. She is widely published locally and nationally in business, health care and consumer magazines and was a guest columnist on health care policy and politics for *The Seattle Times*.

Semi-retired she is now focusing on personal writings, and is working on new collection of poetry and a family memoir, *Last Letters to Ireland*.

COLOPHON

This text was designed and produced in Adobe InDesign by Scott Carnz and printed by CreateSpace on 60# white paper. All photographs are from the author's personal collection and were digitized using Adobe Photoshop.

The body text is set in 10 point Garamond, designed by Adobe; section titles are set in Bell Gothic, designed by Chauncey H. Griffith, and the cover title is set in Amerika, designed by Astrophysics Labs.